Story Numbers

Artistic Writers

1. Dr. Seuss writes poems (poet)
2. The Sherman brothers write songs (songwriter)
3. Jacqueline Woodson writes books (author)
4. Christine French Cully and Judy Burke edit a magazine (editor)
5. Nonny de la Pena writes the news (journalist)
6. ShaoLan Hsueh writes languages (linguist)
7. Mindy Kaling writes comedy (comedian)

Artistic Performers

8. Kid President performs on YouTube (social media star)
9. Rob Paulsen performs as a cartoon (voice actor)
10. Chrissy Metz performs on television (actor)
11. Kristin Chenoweth performs on stage (theater star)
12. Elton John performs on his piano (musician)
13. Antonia Brico leads musical performances (conductor)
14. Cindy Mizelle and Janice Pendarvis perform songs (singers)
15. Caroll Spinney performs inside a puppet (puppeteer)
16. Misty Copeland performs ballet (dancer)
17. Danica Patrick performs in a race car (extreme sports)
18. Usain Bolt performs at the Olympics (athlete)

Artistic Designers

19. Ralph Giles designs cars (designer)
20. Lucas Congdon designs dream backyards (landscape artist)
21. Donna Karan designs what we wear (clothing designer)
22. Joanna Gaines designs rooms (interior decorator)
23. Laolu Senbanjo designs walking art (artist)
24. Kevyn Aucoin designs on faces (makeup artist)
25. Bill Peet designs cartoons (illustrator)
26. Anne Geddes designs pictures (photographer)
27. Barry Sonnenfeld directs movie design (director)
28. Maryann Brandon edits movie design (editor)
29. Es Devlin designs concerts and theaters (stage designer)

By Holly A. Sharp

Dear Dreamers,

What an exciting time to be looking to the future. The world around you is changing faster than it did for your parents or your grandparents. Technology is changing every day, the earth is counting on you, and we are working to be a kinder, more equal human race. You will have a major part in all of that. The question is: what will be your role in this change?

Although these people may have different job titles, they have a few things in common:

1. They didn't just dream about doing something. **They did something about it.**
2. **They didn't wait** until they were a "grownup" to start. They found something they were good at or cared about when they were young and followed it.
3. **They kept going when things were hard**. Many people in this book didn't have easy childhoods or were told they were too different to be successful. They didn't care and let their dreams and hard work lead the way.
4. **They weren't scared of failing**. To do something great means trying. Trying means possibly failing. You may try 99 times and fail, but what if you change the world the 100th time you try?
5. **They cared about the world around them**. It's okay to want to make money. It's okay to want to be famous. It's okay to want to follow a talent you're good at. All of these things just get better when you use your money and talents to improve the world around you as well.

I hope that even just one of these stories makes you curious enough to go out and try something new, explore a talent, or learn more. Each and every one of you has nothing but the future ahead of you and every possibility still remains open, even beyond the 100 in this book. Take advantage of this freedom and explore. Try as much as you can, don't be afraid to fail, and when you find something you love or something you care about, keep doing it.

I would love to hear from you, on social media or by email, about what dreams you have and if you found one in this book.

No matter what, keep dreaming and keep doing.

Holly A. Sharp—author, mother, entrepreneur, brand wizard, inventor, and researcher.

This book is dedicated to the dreamers

The ones who stare out the window and dream about space.
The ones who doodle in their notebooks and dream about characters.
The ones who take apart alarm clocks and dream about robots.
The ones who see a problem and dream of solutions.
The ones who dream of a world better than today.
The ones who dream of equality for all of their friends.
The ones who dream of all the possibilities that lie ahead.
You will be amazing—just go out and do it.

Scott—thank you for dreaming with me and making this possible.
Grammie—thank you for making it possible to dream (and write).
Carrie—There are not enough thank you's in the world for all you have done as my "big sister".
My 3 families—You are big and you are loud and you are the reason I am who I am today.
Ronnie—thank you for being the dream I have been waiting for.
Natalie—thank you for your love of reading and giving me the idea for this dream.
Rehma, Emery, Anthony, Ryder, Walker, and future babies—I hope all of your dreams come true and that this book helps you find those dreams.

All *Dream It & Do It* research was done using only autobiographical materials. Please see the bibliography at www.dreamitandoit.com/bibliography. Role models were chosen that represent the rainbow of children in the world and those that had autobiographical materials available. All due diligence was used to provide only the most accurate information about the job itself and the role model used to highlight the job, however, if you believe there is a detail that deserves further attention, please reach the author at **dreamitanddoitbooks@gmail.com.**

Dream It & Do It – Kid Role Models is launching in the spring of 2021. If you know a child who would be a good role model, share their story on Instagram or Facebook with #dreamit&doit. For updates on this book launch, follow us or join our mail list at **www.dreamitandoit.com.**

FIRST EDITION

Artistic Dreams
WRITERS, PERFORMERS, AND DESIGNERS

Any dream can be creative if you use problem solving and imagination.

The careers in this section are the ones you could dream of getting if you study creative arts. Remember, this is just a sample of jobs that require artistic ability. The opportunity is as wide as you can dream it.

Writers, performers, and designers rely on their imagination, creativity, and craftiness to stand out at what they do.

They also have to work very hard to succeed in their profession. As you'll soon read, these skills require dedication, hard work, and lots of practice.

No matter what dream you have, be proud of ideas that are different.

Dream it and write it
Dream it and perform it
Dream it and design it
And then
Dream It and Do It

Dream of Writing Poems

LIKE

Dr. Seuss

Ted Seuss Guisel, who would come to use the name Dr. Seuss, realized in one single moment that he was meant to be a fantasy storyteller. That one moment was when his future wife peeked into his secret journal and convinced him his imaginary characters and poems were wonderful. She begged him to share his work with others, so he decided to create characters and poems that would entertain children.

Until then, he had loved to draw and write poems, but the adults in his life convinced him that art and poetry were hobbies and that he should be a doctor or at least a more serious writer. In fact, a teacher once told him that he would never succeed because his ideas broke all the rules.

Because of his willingness to keep his writing and characters a secret for so long, Dr. Seuss transformed a hobby into a career. He was working for over ten years before his first book of poems was published.

There were many times during his life when Dr. Seuss could have given up, but he kept working at his craft and getting better and better. He could have become a *real* doctor as his parents wanted. He could have given up when he was hired to draw advertisements. He could have given up when no one would sell his first book, but he kept doing what he loved in his spare time.

The first book he sold was written when Dr. Seuss was traveling on a large boat across the ocean and heard the rhythm of the engine. He liked how the noise sounded and he wrote a story to the beats he heard coming from the ship. This poem-like story would become his first book, *And To Think That I Saw It on Mulberry Street*.

When you think about your favorite Dr. Seuss story, does it surprise you that they were inspired by something like the sound of a boat engine?

This book was rejected twenty-seven times before the twenty-eighth publisher decided to sell it. While this first book did not make a lot of money, people loved it and it led to many more books in the future. Dr. Seuss loved capturing his imagination on paper regardless of whether someone paid him.

He kept writing until he was eighty-six years old, sold hundreds of millions of books, and was awarded a special Pulitzer Prize (which is one of the top awards in writing).

I am sure you know many of his books, such as *Horton Hatches the Egg, The Cat in the Hat, How the Grinch Stole Christmas!, One Fish Two Fish Red Fish Blue Fish, There's a Wocket in my Pocket and Oh, the Places You'll Go!*

While many poets, like Dr. Seuss, turn their poems into books, other poets use their poems to inspire songwriters. After all, many songs are poetry set to music. Poets can even write speeches for people like the President of the United States and other politicians or celebrities.

If you want to become a writer, the best thing you can do is read, practice, and share your writing with others. Get a blank journal or notebook and start writing stories. Share them with family and friends or read them to a librarian or teacher. Think of occasions to celebrate and write a poem about that day.

When you find a sentence you love in a book, copy it down with the name of the original writer. There are also books available called "story starters" that can help give ideas for stories to write. Look back at your journal and see if something that happened in your life could be turned into a story. Keep reading!

Dream of Writing Songs

LIKE

The Sherman Brothers

Songs are like snowflakes, there are millions of them in the world and each one is unique. Each one is made up of only twenty-one notes, but combined in a way that makes it different from every other song written before it.

It is songwriters that are responsible for the words and music that make a song unique. The Sherman Brothers were songwriters that spent their career writing songs for Disney. They wrote for movies like *Mary Poppins*, *Winnie the Pooh*, *Jungle Book*, and *Charlotte's Web*.

The Sherman brothers were very good at using moments in their own life to make songs relatable and fun for both kids and adults. They transformed memories and moments into lyrics that are impossible to resist.

In the movie *Mary Poppins*, there is a song called *Let's go Fly a Kite*. When the movie called for a scene where the kids and their father were to play together, the brothers drew upon their own childhood. The Sherman family always seemed to have their eye on the winds.

Their father loved to build and fly kites and even if they were in the middle of a lesson, their father would hear the wind and jump out of his seat and yell, "let's go fly a kite!" The boys would grab their jackets and kites and follow their father outside, taking advantage of the newly arrived winds. This experience comes alive in the movie when the Banks' children and their usually rigid father fly kites together.

Another song in *Mary Poppins* that the brothers helped to write is called *A Spoonful of Sugar Helps the Medicine Go Down*. The movie called for a song where Mary Poppins helped the children make cleaning their room fun. The brothers were trying to find a catchy way to say that if you add fun to a chore, it becomes less of a chore and more of a game.

As Richard was sitting at the piano trying to write, his son walked in the room having just arrived home from school. Asking about his day, his son revealed that he had to take some bad tasting medicine that day. When asked how he managed it, the son said it wasn't so bad because it was taken with a spoonful of sugar. The next day, Richard and Robert wrote this iconic song.

Much like being a poet or writer, songwriters need to find just the right words to express a moment. However, a songwriter also has to understand music so well that they can set these words to a unique set of notes that people will enjoy listening to. While the Sherman brothers spent their career writing songs for movies, songwriters also work for recording artists, advertising agencies, or theaters.

A fun way to practice the art of songwriting is to take a melody that you already know, like *Twinkle Twinkle Little Star* and come up with something new for the song to be about. Now write a new song setting these new words to fit to the melody. For example: Meow, meow kitty cat, you are very soft and fat… but you'll do much better!

The Sherman brothers were good at writing songs that people could relate to because they drew stories from their own lives. Making up silly songs can be fun and a good way to get started, but the more serious you become about song writing, the more you should practice writing songs that will touch people. Keep a journal to write down thoughts you have or lines that you find catchy. Just like all these writing jobs, whatever you do, just keep writing.

Dream of Writing Books

LIKE

Jacqueline Woodson

Writers have a super power. They can do something that no one else can. They can transport you from a cozy chair in your living room to far off worlds. They can introduce you to people so real, you feel as though you have always known them.

Jacqueline understood this power at a young age. She would tell her friends "story-lies" and watch their faces light up because they believed her tales. The power of storytelling took over her life and she would write stories all over the place. Sometimes, grownups wouldn't appreciate the places she chose to document her stories, like the side of a building. But this didn't stop her. She kept on writing.

When she was in elementary school she started submitting the stories that she wrote. She won an award for one of the first stories she shared. That is when she realized that while lies told out loud get you in trouble, lies told on paper win you awards. Make-believe is acceptable when they're written storytelling.

Jacqueline kept reading and writing as she grew. Her first book was about the friendship of two eleven-year-old girls and the struggle of growing up. Someone heard her story at a public reading and loved it so much that they helped her to sell it.

As a writer, Jacqueline wants her writing to help people have conversations about the world. She uses her super power to help people feel less alone. Her stories are about situations that people experience but have a hard time talking about.

One book called *The Day You Begin* is about being new and different. People, especially young people, feel different for lots of reasons. Because people are different from each other, there will always be something that makes us feel like we don't belong. Jacqueline uses her story to make people who feel different realize that many people feel this way. She reflects on the lessons of her own life and encourages readers to "tell your story" and to help others understand you better. This will help you feel a little less different.

Jacqueline writes books for people of all ages with the goal of using her stories and characters to help make the world a more open and understanding place.

She says, "Books give people a place to go to begin a conversation. Books help us to get us to talk and take the fear out of hard conversations."

Jacqueline believes that good writing starts with a lot of reading. She credits her love of writing to the hours she would spend in her room reading, even when she could hear the laughter of her friends playing outside in the street. If you think writing books could be a career that you are interested in, push yourself to read as many different types of books as possible. Ask your teacher or librarian for advice on advanced books that will introduce you to topics, like the ones in Jacqueline's books, that make you think and have challenging conversations.

Dream of Editing a Magazine

LIKE

Judy Burke and Christine French Cully

Do you keep a scrapbook of your favorite pictures or maybe of a family vacation? How do you decide which pictures to include? How do you decide what order to put them in? Do you include captions? Do you include decorative stickers or paper to enhance the visual presentation of your photos? If so, you are already an editor in the making! Christine French Cully and Judy Burke are editors for the magazine *Highlights.*

This is one of the longest-running children's magazines in the world. You may have a subscription or may have seen one in your school or doctor's office.

Christine and Judy work together to shape the experience that children have when they read *Highlights* magazine. Their goal is to create a magazine that helps children have fun with a purpose. Judy says, "I know that my nine-year-old self would be excited that I work at *Highlights.*"

It takes nearly a year to plan out what will go in each issue, which is delivered every month. This is because they plan everything that will be written, oversee the research and writing of the stories, have the pictures drawn, lay out the entire issue, and then edit the magazine for mistakes.

A retired couple wanting a second career started *Highlights* magazine seventy years ago. So, your grandparents, parents and hopefully, kids like you, have read it. One of the things that make *Highlights* special is that in all the years that they have been writing for children, they personally answer every single letter that they get in the mail. Christine says, "I love reading and answering kids' mail. What they tell us is beautiful and I think kids really benefit from our personalized responses."

Some of the characters and games in *Highlights* have been in the magazine since the beginning. For example, *Goofus and Gallant* is a comic that tells a story about good choices and bad choices. There have been over eight hundred different stories about these two kids. Each month, Judy sits with her team and has to think about a new story and how it will fit with the theme of that issue. This is true for the seek-and-find, the *Ask Arizona* advice column and the other stories included.

Every book and magazine has an editor who makes sure that the publication has the right look and feel before anyone gets to read it. So, maybe you are interested in sports – could you be the next editor for *Sports Illustrated?* If you like music, maybe your calling is to be an editor at *Rolling Stone.* There are magazines about travel, crafting, movies, cooking, news, and so many other things that people care about.

Christine and Judy both care about children. They believe that kids are the most important people in the whole world. Judy says, "We care about the whole child, not just to teach them things. We want them to learn and grow emotionally, deal with the things that come up in life, and to grow socially. We look at kids and ask how we help them become better versions of themselves."

When you care about something so much, it is easy to love working on it and thinking about it every day. You can start your own magazine about a topic you care about, sharing the project with your friends and family. Think about including articles, games, photographs, drawings, and maybe an advice column.

Dream of Writing the News

LIKE

Nonny de la Peña

Can you name five major events happening in the world today? It could be major news like a presidential election. Or, it could be news closer to home, like the local basketball team winning the state championship. How we learn about events happening all over the world, or right next-door, is through journalism. Journalists learn the details of a story and tell it to us through news shows, newspapers, magazines, podcasts, or social media. Nonny de la Peña is helping to create a new form of journalism that might be common by the time you are older – virtual reality news.

Nonny learned at a very young age that there are many sides to any story. When she was in middle school, her teacher sent a note home for something disruptive she had done in class- like interrupting the teacher. When the note reached her father, he sat her down at the kitchen table, showed her the note and said, "This is what your teacher said you did." Then, he turned the piece of paper over and surprised her by saying, "Now, I want to write down the facts of your side of the story." So, Nonny was able to tell her father what she felt had happened without first getting in trouble. "Now," he said, "you can see there are many sides to every story." It seemed to her that a story is about understanding different points of view.

Nonny spent many years studying communication and journalism and wrote for many famous newspapers, magazines, and TV shows. However, she felt some stories were not getting enough attention because they were harder for people to relate to, like hunger. Nonny felt that it was a big problem that food banks in the United States were running out of food for people who needed it, but she couldn't get people to read her stories or care.

She heard about a man who was waiting in line for food and was so hungry that he fell over, and someone had to call an ambulance because of his hunger. Then, she had a thought: "What if I could present this story and have people remember it with their entire body, and not just their mind?" By creating a news story that looks like a virtual reality video game, people watching the story would feel like they were standing in line waiting for food. They could see the man faint from hunger. They could hear the panic as people were trying to figure out what to do.

It was a much more powerful story when you feel as though you are witnessing it happen before your eyes. After word spread about the power of her storytelling through virtual reality, she was asked to tell stories about lots of other topics that people hear about but have a hard time relating to, like war.

"We are still following the same principals of traditional journalism," Nonny says when talking about whether her style of reporting is too different. "What is different is that you have a sense of being on the scene. I've had people tell me that as a result of watching our story, they have turned around and donated to a local food pantry. That's money right out of their bank account. Clearly, this has had an impact. This is a new form of doing journalism that is going to join all the normal platforms in the future."

You don't have to be super high-tech like Nonny to be a journalist. In fact, it is best to start with the basics. The best way to practice your journalism skills is to interview people and find an interesting story to tell. Get a notebook and find someone to talk to. Ask them questions about either a specific topic you want to report on or talk to them until you find something interesting – and then keep digging. Write up your story and share it with others. Put a collection of stories together to make your own newspaper. Maybe it's a family newspaper about all of your different family members. Maybe it is a neighborhood newspaper about the people and things happening on your street or in your school. There are a set of books called *The Newspaper Club* that you could probably find at your local library which will help teach you about being a kid journalist.

Dream of Writing (and Speaking) Languages

LIKE

ShaoLan Hseuh

There is almost no skill as powerful as knowing another language. It opens up parts of the world, relationships with people, and opportunities. You can be a translator and help people who speak different languages have a conversation, you can work in a foreign country, or you can work in the travel industry; the possibilities are endless, as it literally opens the world up to you.

English is not the most spoken language in the world. That would be Mandarin, the language that is spoken in China.

ShaoLan loved the language so much that she developed a system to help people learn to read her beautiful language.

ShaoLan grew up in Taiwan in a family that loved the art of calligraphy (drawing letters in a fancy way). Her grandfather was a professional calligrapher. ShaoLan and her mother would spend hours together with nothing but an ink brush and paper, drawing Chinese characters.

Unlike the English alphabet, which has twenty-six letters that make up all of the words, Mandarin has thousands of characters. Each word is its own character. So, to be able to write this language, you have to learn the character for each word. Starting at the age of five, ShaoLan would practice her characters, getting them perfect and learning a new one each day for fifteen years.

ShaoLan loved to draw these characters, but when she moved away from Taiwan and had children of her own, she was having a hard time motivating them to learn the characters of her home language.

She realized that the normal person does not need to know the twenty thousand characters that were possible to learn. To have basic skills, you only need to know a few hundred.

So, she chose the most useful words that people needed to know and created pictures out of them that make you think of the word that they stand for.

For example, the word "mouth" is a square-shaped character. She added lips and teeth to the character to help you remember this shape is like an open mouth.

She draws the word fire to look like a person yelling "help me, I am on fire!" Then, she teaches you how to put them together.

Once you learn fire and you learn mountain, the symbol for volcano is fire and mountain put together.

ShaoLan took all of these pictures and created an app called Chineasy that allows people to easily learn on their phone. Her app is now used by thousands of people and received a lot of awards for helping make a complicated topic easier.

There is proof that it is easier to learn languages while you are young than it is when you are older. There are lots of ways to learn a new language. There are apps like Chineasy, there are online lessons like muzzybbc.com and LittlePim.com, or you can just go to YouTube and type in the language you want to learn and you will find lots of videos in dual languages.

Dream of Writing Comedy
LIKE
Mindy Kaling

You can be a joke teller when you grow up. No joke!

Mindy Kaling wasn't the class clown when she was in school, but she loved comedy. Comedy movies, comedy shows, and comedy skits—you name it. Mindy embraced her love of comedy and surrounded herself with friends who also liked to make people laugh. Those friends helped her to become a famous comedian who both acted in and wrote for several of the most popular comedies on television today.

Her first year of high school, Mindy had a secret friend, Mavis. Mavis and Mindy bonded over comedy. It didn't matter if it was good or bad; they loved it all. They were comedy nerds and just loved watching and talking about it nonstop. They would spend entire days and nights in the family living room watching as much as they could. More than just watching though, they loved reenacting certain scenes. Mavis, however, was her secret friend because her at-school friends were the ones she had known for most of her life and hung out with every day. But they didn't love comedy the way that Mindy did.

One night her "at-school" friends came over and wanted to watch a serious movie while Mindy wanted to share one of her and Mavis's favorite comedies. Her friends didn't think the movie was funny. She had known that her school-friends didn't love comedy in the same way, but seeing them miss the humor in this funny movie made her feel like she was two different people, one with Mavis and one with them.

Mindy believes that what happened to her is something that happens to a lot of professional comedy writers or comedians, or really anyone who's passionate about anything and discovering it for the first time. She says, "Most people who do what I do are obsessed with comedy, especially when we are young."

More and more Mindy found that she didn't want to do what her "at-school" friends wanted to do. They became interested in sewing and horses and Mindy wanted to spend her time with Mavis. "I didn't want her to be my secret friend anymore." By the end of the year, it was just the two of them. Mavis helped her learn about who she wanted to be. I love comedy and now I surround myself with people who love to talk about it just as much as I do."

Looking back, Mindy is glad she was an outsider who obsessed over comedy with Mavis. She tells young people, "Don't peak in high school. Don't worry about being super popular. Almost no one who was a big star in high school is also a big star later in life. I was never the lead in the play. Because I was largely overlooked at school, I watched everyone like an observant weirdo. It has helped me so much as a writer, and you have no idea. I just want ambitious teenagers to know that it is totally fine to be quiet, observant kids. "So many people I work with, famous actors and accomplished writers, were overlooked in high school. Sit next to the class clown and study him. Then grow up, take everything you learned, and get paid to be a real-life clown."

In college, Mindy found a friend like Mavis, someone with a shared sense of humor named Brenda. After college, they struggled to find work writing or acting until they created a play to perform themselves. Mindy and Brenda wrote it, had a friend produce it, and put up flyers everywhere to get people to come see it. Their play was entered into a contest and was named the best new play out of the 500 that were entered. This is how Mindy met the people who asked her to write for a hit comedy show. She worked to be noticed instead of waiting for the right person to hire her.

As you continue to grow up and make more friends, don't be afraid to make new friends that like the same things you like, even if that means hanging out with a new group of people. You never know where these friendships will lead. If you're interested in practicing comedy, try this simple storytelling game. Comedy is just about telling funny stories. Sit in a circle and have someone start a story. The next person repeats the story and adds to it. Keep going until you can't add any more details.

Dream of Performing on YouTube

LIKE

Robby Novak (Kid President)

You probably know someone in your life that always seems to be posing for the camera. They won't put their phone down until they get just the right picture. They want to give off the impression that their life is perfect so that they seem cool online. YouTube might give the impression that the stars have perfect lives or that it's easy. Neither is true. Robby Novak became a massive YouTube star by doing what this book encourages you to do—playing and exploring different choices. He did it without being fake and just being himself.

It all started when Robby made one video at the request of his brother-in-law (Brad) and found something that that people enjoyed viewing. In the summer of 2012, the country was in the middle of a presidential election, causing a lot of heated debate between people. The idea for a "Kid President" came from a playful idea that putting something online would help lessen political debate. It'd be funny and uplifting, or at least something to do on a boring afternoon.

Robby said, "I didn't think that the world needed a kid as president of the United States. I just thought that world needed grown-ups to pause and see things through the eyes of a kid."

Robby's first video was just for fun. The studio consisted of a presidential seal drawn on a large piece of cardboard, a record player as a desk, two American flags held up with duct tape, and a nameplate that said "President."

Without really writing anything down or practicing, Robby was told, "You're the president, this is your chance to tell all the grown-ups of the world what you want them to hear." So he did. He made his first video with Brad, who loved it so much he wondered, "What if a kid told everybody what he or she thought? What if that kid was Robby? Would anyone hear a happy, small voice over the louder, older, angry ones?"

What makes Robby special and such a beloved YouTube star (his most viewed video has over 45 million views!) was that his goal was never about becoming famous. His message is about what can we accomplish. He wanted to spread joy and help other kids be awesome. In fact, the reason that a group called "Soul Pancake" stepped in to make him more famous was they felt the Internet needed more joy. Most of his videos AND his book *The Kid President's Guide to Being Awesome* are almost exclusively focused on the 100 ideas he has for people to spread joy.

Titles of his most popular videos are *A pep talk from kid president to you, 20 things we should say more often, 25 reasons to be thankful,* and *An open letter to Moms.* Robby also created the idea of "day making"—changing the world through making someone's day. For example, he created Socktober, in October, to donate socks to homeless shelters. He also had a parade for his town's mailwoman. As a result of these videos, kids from around the world have engaged with Kid President to do awesome things of their own. For example, one of his viewers threw a "be awesome" birthday party where his guests brought him supplies for school that they donated to kids in need. Acts like these from kids all over the country make each neighborhood a better place to live. Both Kid President and his followers are proof that you don't have to be a grown-up to make a difference.

As a result of his YouTube fame, Robby has been on talk shows, met President Obama, kissed Beyoncé, and interviewed countless celebrities. However, he has only used his access to fame to spread the word about making the world more awesome.

If you have dreams of being a YouTube star, think less about what you can do to be famous and more about what you can do to make a difference where you live. Is there someone you can celebrate, someone you can help, questions you can ask, or something that would cause people to laugh, dance, or smile? Make a video about that and worry later about if people would like it. Remember to always get your parents' permission before ever posting something online! Take Robby's advice: "Be yourself. Everyone else is taken."

Dream of Performing as a Cartoon

LIKE

Rob Paulsen

Rob Paulsen moved to California right after college with the dream of becoming a singer or movie star. His dream of becoming a voice-over actor started only when he was given a job on the show *GI Joe*, which was his very first voice acting audition! Voice actors provide the voices for your favorite TV and movie cartoon characters. Not only do they have to act, but they often also sing and make silly voices as well. Rob's passion and talent grew over time because he learned to love how silly and creative he was allowed to be in his job.

During his career, Rob played characters on *GI Joe, Teenage Mutant Ninja Turtles, Veggie Tales, Animaniacs,* and dozens of other animated television series. He was able to get into the world of voice acting using his training in singing and performing, but also because he was willing to be silly. At one point in his career, Rob was very sick and unable to use his voice well but he still remained playful, relying on humor to get through his illness. He says that some of the most talented voice actors were able to "unlearn adult behavior," meaning that they relearn to be silly and not worry about what others think.

As you grow older, adults try hard to fit in and it makes it hard to be silly in front of others. For adults doing voice-overs for cartoons, a sense of humor needs to be very strong. Rob was willing to be funny while working really hard. Not taking yourself too seriously is a valuable skills.

Rob continued working, he became known for his fearlessness and silliness as much as his voice skills. He says, "My skill was lack of fear first." He would try anything with his voice. He loved playing his characters and "doing voices" for his friends and family. Whether it was saying "cowabunga dude" to his son's friends or children he would meet at comic book festivals, or making Animaniac jokes for strangers in restaurants and hotels, he used his voice to make people laugh.

Imagine if you were working at a restaurant and were taking someone's order and all of a sudden recognized the voice of one of your favorite cartoon characters. Voice actors don't have famous faces like other types of actors, but they certainly do have famous voices.

This made Rob realize that maybe people would want to hear HIM talk about the characters and be silly outside of the cartoon world. He was right. Today, he performs his *Anamaniacs* songs in concert for people all over the United States and has a popular voice-over podcast.

For Rob, it didn't matter whether he was 22 years old and the new guy in the room or in his 60s performing in front of a huge studio audience. Staying real and searching for ways to make people laugh is his whole job. How wonderful to have a job doing the things that most kids get in trouble for doing in school today!

If you want to be a voice actor like Rob Paulsen, you should practice crazy voices in front of others. A fun way to practice your new hobby is to find different stuffed animals and action figures and give them a personality. Ask someone to record you giving each of these characters a different voice. Then play the video back and listen. Do the voices sound different? What makes each one special?

Remember that it's okay to be as silly as you can be!

Dream of Performing as a TV Actor

LIKE

Chrissy Metz

Performing in TV and movies means learning lines and pretending to be a different person on a regular basis. Chrissy Metz fell in love with getting to be someone else. Chrissy loved to sing and make people laugh and dreamt of being an entertainer from a very young age. Sometimes people were unkind to her because of how she looked.

Chrissy struggled with her weight, which made her feel different and have less confidence. A boy that she liked was only nice to her in secret. Looking back, Chrissy said, "I didn't feel safe showing vulnerability, so I did it all alone. It's ironic, because now showing vulnerability is all I do in my work."

Because her confidence was low when she was young, Chrissy didn't show off her talent for singing or acting in front of many people. She worked on increasing her confidence in unusual places. For example, when she worked at the McDonalds drive through she said, "I saw the drive-thru as a chance to connect with people, even if only for eleven seconds. It was like a performance, where I could do off-kilter voices at the microphone. On nights, I'd entertain with my English accent with a touch of class."

When she was a teenager, she took her younger sisters and her friends to a talent search in their town, but her belief in herself was not enough to audition. When one of the judges asked her if she was there to audition, she responded by saying, "I would love to sing, but…" and trailed off her words, scared to really answer. The woman pushed her to sing something. Chrissy did and was chosen as a winner. This audition led her to join a group that later drove to California to audition for parts in TV shows and movies.

When they arrived in Hollywood where most TV shows and movies are made, Chrissy struggled to get parts. Casting agents told her she had to lose weight or accept being the joke of the show. There were few opportunities in Hollywood for plus-sized women. She thought, "As a plus-size woman, how am I going to do this? Do I, or can I, conform? Why am I relegated to my dress size? I had to stop caring about what I wasn't and focus on what I was: courageous, committed and willing to sacrifice for something I wanted."

This courage is what makes Chrissy so special and such a great actor. She learned to love herself and believe that she was enough, no matter what others said. She lived by the words of a wise man named Gandhi, "No one can hurt me without my permission." For almost 10 years she kept trying to find an acting job. She says, "Our true happiness is inside of us. Like me, everything you need to fly, to soar, has been inside of you all along. Just as you are, *you're enough*. It was only once I stopped looking outside for people to approve of me, and looked inward instead, that I realized I have all I need to fly."

Despite the bullying or being told she wasn't the right size for an actor, Chrissy had the confidence to become an actor because she felt acting was a way that she could play a part and connect with people. "As an actor, I got to be another person and relate to her plight."

Now she is on one of the most successful TV shows about the life of a family. Chrissy loves acting because, "You must stay present. You can't worry about the next scene because you're in one this moment. It's the same thing with our lives. Just play the scene and see where it takes you."

At any age, you can take acting lessons, however, if you are dreaming of becoming an actor, Chrissy would tell you, "You really must love it, because that love is going to get you through the hard times and the long hours—and lots of auditions!"

Dream of Performing on Stage

LIKE

Kristin Chenoweth

One of the things that makes New York City special is a street called Broadway. So many famous theaters are located on this street! If you are lucky and talented enough to perform in one of these theaters, you are a "Broadway star." You don't, however, need to be on Broadway to be in the theater. Kristin Chenoweth spent many years touring all over the United States performing in many different theaters and television shows before she called Broadway home.

Kristin's journey to Broadway started when she was four. While watching television, she saw a ballerina dancing and that was all it took. Her mother enrolled her in ballet classes and Kristin was immediately dedicated to becoming the best ballerina she could possibly be. It didn't come easily as she was small for her age and dancing is hard work. Once, she tried out for a role in *The Nutcracker* and was certain she wouldn't get the role. Kristin felt that, "I was fully prepared to be told I was too little. Too little was something I heard a lot. I didn't want to be taller just for the sake of being the same as everyone else. I was just tired of looking at butts all the time!" She did end up getting the role but found that while dancing didn't come naturally to her, singing did.

Kristin remained "short", but she quickly adds that, "Life is short while she is not. So do the things you enjoy doing!" This is one of the most important lessons that Kristin teaches to her young fans and future Broadway hopefuls. You shouldn't do theater because it seems glamorous or you could be famous. Do it because you have fun singing and performing in front of people and couldn't imagine doing anything else. To become the singer she is today, Kristin studied singing for six years, lived in a one-bedroom apartment with four other people, and took jobs far away from home trying to get her big break. It was always hard work, but also fun.

Have you ever heard of the musical, *Annie*, about a redheaded orphan adopted by the wealthy Daddy Warbucks? Kristin was a finalist for the original *Annie* movie, not because she was a professional actress, but because she was talented and having fun, and it showed. When she arrived at the audition, she looked around and realized the other children had professional pictures and people managing them. Many of them were very serious and did not seem like they were having fun at all. "What is the point of dedicating your life to something if you aren't having any fun?" she thought. Her Mom and Dad, who knew nothing about the acting world, felt the same way and encouraged her to be happy. If she was happy singing and dancing for an audience, they supported her.

One job she took because it was so much fun (versus popular) was a musical called *Wicked*, a musical about the witches of the *Wizard of Oz.*, It took 3 years to develop before it had an audience and even longer before it was playing on Broadway. During this time, Kristin turned down other roles because she loved the role of Glinda the Good Witch so much. Today *Wicked* is one of Broadway's longest running musicals. It made over 1 BILLION dollars and won countless awards.

Being a theater star, especially a musical theater star, requires lots of skills like the ability to act, dance, and sing. There is a lot of work required to be good at all 3, but it's important to have fun along the way. If you are interested in musical theater, go to live theater or a filmed musical and watch for the different skills the actors use. There are tons of musicals made for kids, just ask your parents to help you find one. Why not start with *Annie*? The remake actually has Kristin in the cast.

Dream of Performing as a Musician

LIKE

Elton John

Elton John was born a natural musician. There are legends in his family, of him sitting on his aunt's lap at the piano, age three, playing a song on his own. As he grew older, this love of music continued to grow, especially for a style of music called Rock and Roll. His mother brought home a new record every Friday, back when you could only buy music on vinyl records from record stores. Elton said that waiting for her to get home to see what record she chose was his favorite time of the week.

While singing or playing an instrument for a living sounds like fun, it's also hard work. By the age of 12 he was entered into a special school for gifted musicians that he attended on the weekends. Elton says, "I was just born with a good ear, the way some people are born with a photographic memory. If I heard something once, I could go to the piano and, more or less, play it perfectly." Even though he had an amazing gift and was taking classes to get even better, he still had to work hard to convince people that he could be a rock and roll star.

He had to discover the best way to use his talents to make people want to listen to him play. Making friends with Bernie Taupin, a man who was equally as talented at setting words to music, changed his life. Together Elton and Bernie would write hundreds of songs. Bernie would write the words and Elton would add the music. Sometimes they created a hit song on their first try.

One day when Bernie and Elton were working together to create a new song, Bernie wrote down all the words to a song called "Your Song" while eating breakfast. By the time he was done eating, he handed the words to Elton who sat down at the piano and started playing. Fifteen minutes later, they had created one of the most popular songs they would write together. This magic continued for over 30 years. Elton says, "Bernie writes the words and gives them to me, I read them, play a chord and something else takes over and comes through my fingers."

Elton proved this to be true when he was performing one day for a show called *Inside the Actors Guild,* he asked someone in the audience for a book. He looked at the words at the start of a random chapter, sat down at the piano, and wrote a brand new song with words he had never seen before!

Think about this: if you learn to play guitar, it's a good skill to have, but would you really want to just play alone? Your musical talent is more valuable when you work with other musicians. Collaborating with a fellow artist can take good to great. In some cases it might be to write songs, like Elton and Bernie or it might be to create music with other instruments or it might be to partner with a singer. Even when Elton was asked to sing and create music for the Disney musical, *Lion King,* he had to work with many other musicians to help develop the final product.

If you love music the way that Elton does, you don't have to have his genius-level talent, but you need to be willing to put in the time to practice and want to collaborate with others the way he did. The best way to really invest in learning an instrument is to take lessons, but more and more it is possible to do this over the computer or through videos instead of having to invest in in-person lessons. No matter how you do it, music requires practice, practice, practice!

Dream of Leading Musical Performances

LIKE

Antonia Brico

Antonia dreamed of being a conductor when she was a young girl and she often went to the park on Sunday afternoons to watch bands play. Staring at the conductor, it seemed that he was holding a magic wand. The man standing in front of the band would wave that wand and the band would respond with their music. Even though it was just a little stick, Antonia was in love.

This love for conducting started when she was 10 and bit her nails. The doctor told her stepmother that learning to play the piano might help her to stop. Right away she was a natural. People said she could, "play in the dark." Playing the piano not only worked but started a life-long love of the instrument and, eventually, conducting. A conductor is the person who stands facing an orchestra directing how they should play together. During practice, the conductor gives the different musicians instructions on how to play so that the music sounds as special as possible.

This was a big deal because Antonia was a girl. Before her, there were only a few female conductors in the world. She fell in love with a job that the man in the park, she used to watch as child, told her was not a job for women. Luckily, Antonia was a special girl. She strongly believed, "If you are meant to do something, take the first step. If it works out, the other steps will follow." She took the first step and tried.

An example of this willingness to try happened before anyone knew her as a conductor. She met a very famous piano player and asked him if he might help her find a band to conduct. His response was, "How can I help you if I have never heard you conduct?" Well, conducting a band is not like playing an instrument because it requires people, instruments, and a space. *So*, she thought, *what's the first step?*

I need to hold a concert and be sure he is invited. Antonia found out when this famous person would be in town, used her own money to find a location and hired enough musicians to invite him to her concert. Imagine his surprise when he found out that he was the only person invited! He was so pleased, that he called his friends to tell them about this talented woman conductor. She was invited to come and conduct bands all over Europe as a result.

Another time that Antonia decided to take a first step, not knowing where it would lead, was when she started the first ever female orchestra. She was conducting a small group of nine women who often played together for fun and small events. This made her ask, "If nine women could play together, why not 90?" Antonia went to the newspaper and took out an ad asking for women who wanted to join her in starting an all female orchestra. As it turned out, in New York where she lived, there were a lot of female musicians who wanted to be a part of her orchestra and she successfully assembled an all-women concert.

Conducting is a special way to have a career in music because you learn to read music, understand all the instruments that you would direct, how music sounds when played correctly, and how to work with lots of different people. If you like listening to music and can identify all the separate parts, you might have a future as a conductor. You can be like Antonia and take a first step by learning to read music. With this skill you can sing, play, or conduct which means that the orchestra follows your lead.

Dream of Performing as a Singer

LIKE

Cindy Mizelle and Janice Pendarvis

You can make a living being a singer in many ways. One way that can be very rewarding is to be a backup singer like Cindy Mizelle, and Janice Pendarvis.

A backup singer's job is to sing the music that compliments the song. Elton John recorded the song "Circle of Life" from the opening of *The Lion King* for the movie's soundtrack. There are backup singers that support him during the song singing lines like, "*Nants ingonyama bagithi Baba Sithi uhm ingonyama,*" which in Zulu means "Here comes a lion father, oh yes it's a lion."

These singers are responsible for singing backup music for important parts of songs when they are being recorded in a studio or when the artist who sings the song is on tour. Many of these singers work with some of the most famous singers in the world and travel to far off places to perform. They get the joy of singing popular songs or seeing the world without having to manage some of the difficult parts of fame.

Cindy Mizelle learned to sing harmonies in church. She loved it so much that she would record herself on 3 different recorders to create a harmonic sound. She began touring when she was only 17 years old and since then has performed with many famous singers and has toured for 5 years with a rockstar called Bruce Springsteen. She loves being a backup singer because, "I can be different people, like a chameleon. You can change it up and you are never bored."

Janice Pendarvis started her life very shy. As a songwriter, she chose to write the songs that other people sing. However, people kept asking her to sing her own songs, so she finally gave in. She has worked with many famous artists and can be heard in the background of some of the most famous songs on the radio today. She says, "When you think about the hooks on your favorite songs, hooks are short, catchy musical phrases, that you love to sing along to. Most of the time, that's us, the backup singer, because that's what we do—sing the hooks."

To become any type of singer, whether a solo singer, backup singer, wedding singer, Broadway singer, or contract singer on a cruise ship, you should practice being comfortable singing in front of people.

If you need to work up your courage to sing in front of people, consider a membership to a voice lesson website. An example of this is yousician.com. You can get lessons and feedback in order to gain confidence. If being a backup singer like Cindy and Janice is attractive to you, you can also use lessons to learn to sing harmonies, which is an important skill if you want to be able to sing with others.

You can arrange a concert for your family, friends or neighborhood and practice what it feels like to sing in front of an audience. There are many ways to do what you love as a singer. If singing is what you love, practice, work hard, and you will find a way!

Dream of Performing as a Puppet

LIKE

Caroll Spinney

Some of your favorite characters on television, like Big Bird on Sesame Street, need humans to help them move and operate. These people are called puppeteers. Caroll Spinney was the man that brought life to Big Bird. He's the only person who operated Big Bird for 50 years. Caroll has been a part of Sesame Street since your parents were children.

When Caroll was a little boy, he saw his first puppet show and it was love at first sight. He bought some used puppets with his own money and began charging neighborhood kids to come to his shows. Caroll learned something important, "Everyone went away smiling and I thought, I am going to be a puppeteer when I grow up!" His Mom was an artist and encouraged him to keep working on his puppet shows, helping him make puppets and buying him his first professional set. "Little did she know she was giving me my career," says Caroll describing how his mother supported his childhood dream.

Caroll did something really special with his dream. He lived it.

As he grew up, he didn't leave his love for puppets behind. He continued improving as a puppeteer as he grew older, even when kids around him made fun of him for "playing with dolls." He would think to himself, "One day I hope these kids will brag that they knew me."

He entered the air force after high school. When he left at the age of 23, he didn't question what he wanted from life. He would continue to work with puppets.

It was one very lucky day, when Caroll was performing a puppet show for a large room of people at a puppet festival, that would change his life forever. Crouched behind the stage, holding onto his puppets, he could feel the bright lights shining down on him. Suddenly he thought, "These lights are shining too bright!" The overhead lights were so bright that they made the background of his show disappear. He wasn't able to deliver his show the way he wanted, but Jim Henson (the creator of *The Muppets* and *Sesame Street*) was in the audience and saw Carroll had talent as a puppeteer and asked him to come to *Sesame Street* and give life to the characters of Big Bird and Oscar.

You might think that bringing a puppet character to life is an easy job, but you have to perform many jobs at once to be successful. To wear Big Bird, Carroll used one hand in the head that weighed five pounds, the weight of an iron. His other hand operated BOTH of Big Bird's arms. Because Carroll did not have his own head inside of Big Bird's head, he could not see outside while he was inside, so there was a camera inside of the Puppet. This meant that Carroll had to be able to act, move Big Bird with his own body, and watch the outside world from a camera, all at the same time. He would do this for every TV show and live appearance from his 30s all the way until he was in his 80s.

If you have a dream or a hobby you love, remember Big Bird and Carroll. Carroll didn't let anyone tell him that his dreams were silly or childish and stuck with them long after he became a grownup. If you have dreams of being a puppeteer, you can practice like Caroll did by buying or making your own puppets and putting on shows. Today, the Jim Henson company that produces shows like *Sesame Street* is looking for new talent. If you get good enough, you can send a video of your show. (Henson.com/employment)

Dream of Performing as Dancer

LIKE

Misty Copeland

Misty Copeland is not only an extremely talented ballerina, but she's the first Black female principal dancer at the famous American Ballet Theater. All dancers must work very hard, from a young age, to become skilled enough to dance professionally. Practicing 6 days a week for many hours a day. Misty not only had to work hard, but she had to do so while struggling with her family not having much money and people holding her back because of the color of her skin.

When Misty was a young girl, she sat flipping through the channels on her television looking for something to watch. She stopped when she saw gymnastics on TV for the first time. She closely watched what they did and then mimicked their movements. She had no idea until later in life that this ability to mimic moves she saw would turn her into a star. She spent hours after school and on weekends copying what she saw and making up routines in her bedroom, pretending she was directing a music video. Most professional ballerinas start dancing with a dance class when they are still in grade school. However, Misty came from a large family without the budget to pay for classes and costumes needed to perform. She kept her dancing a secret, something she did to escape the stresses of her life at home.

Her talent would not stay hidden forever. When Misty was 13 years old, she joined a club at school where she could start dancing with others. One day as she was packing up to go home, her coach pulled her aside and told her, "You know you have the perfect physique for ballet and a natural ability. I know you go to Boys and Girls club after school. A friend of mine teaches a ballet class there. Why don't you check it out?"

It didn't take long for her talent to equal that of other kids who had been dancing for years before her. The real struggle of her dancing career was facing the comments of people who didn't believe ballerinas should be anything but white. Misty would say, "There are people who will just never want to see me dance because of my race. No matter what I do or how I do it, they won't like me." Being judged for her race and not her dancing made Misty feel hurt and angry.

One day an article titled "Where Are All the Black Swans" helped Misty feel better. The article questioned why there weren't more people of color in the world of ballet. Misty felt the article reflected how she was feeling, "There were many people who seemed to not to want to see Black ballerinas, who thought that our very presence made ballet less authentic, less romantic, less true." However, when she went to class, her friends dismissed the article and called it dumb! If her friends couldn't understand her struggle, who would?

Misty knew that she had to find people to talk to outside of her dancing family, a support system like the one she had as a young dancer. She connected with other dancers who had the same struggles and found her strength. They told her, "Walk into a room, knowing you are somebody, somebody special. Don't ever let them smash that or pull you down."

As Misty's confidence grew, she was able to start asking for the things she felt she deserved. She was driven to keep working hard and fighting for good roles, even if it took longer because she believed, "If this could open doors for Black women in ballet, that would mean the world to me. It would all be worth it. That's what I'm doing this for. Not just for my own pleasure and gratification. I need to remember this every morning I wake up tired, just thinking of what I could do, not just for me but for others that come after me."

You are the "others" that Misty worked so hard for. The next generation of dancers who will help open all forms of dance to all different types of people. There are many types of jobs you can do as a dancer. You can be in a ballet company like Misty, perform in theater troupes, dance in music videos, or choreograph other dancers. All these professions demand hard work and require taking many different types of classes to find which kind is perfect for you. If you are interested in dancing as a profession, go and take a class or two! Remember, places like the Boys and Girls clubs, your community center, and YMCA make it possible for anyone to get moving. So go out there and do it!

Dream of Performing an Extreme Sport

LIKE

Danica Patrick

Extreme sports are different from other sports like baseball and basketball because they demand high risk to perform them. You might like watching extreme sports because of how fast they are. Racing, surfing, skateboarding, skydiving, mountain climbing, snowboarding, and biking are exciting to watch. Because people enjoy watching these types of sports, skilled athletes can make money doing them. Danica Patrick is one of the most successful women in American open-wheeled racing, an extreme racing sport where people drive as fast as they possibly can!

A friend of the family owned a go-kart, and when Danica and her sister tried it, they begged their parents for go-karts of their own. Danica quickly realized how much she loved driving and started competing. At her first competition, she was rounding a corner and as she felt the car speeding up, she went for the break. She couldn't get it to work and saw the wall coming closer and closer. She wasn't able to stop the car and was in her first crash.

Thankfully she wasn't hurt, so the next weekend she was excited to get back in her kart and try again. She found that each week she was getting better and better and winning more and more races. By the end of her 22nd race, she came in second place and was determined to keep racing to keep getting better.

Once she made up her mind to compete at racing, she didn't care that this was not a sport that women played. When she was in high school, she was invited to England to race against all boys. Her dad reminded her that, "Don't be the fastest girl, be the fastest person." When she arrived, the boys weren't very nice. Guys were there from all over the world and were not expecting to be beaten by a girl! She would hold her head up high and think, "If I am going to win the Indy 500 one day, I have to do all of this, and I am happy to."

When Danica came back to America, she still faced men who didn't think a woman belonged in a race car, so Danica decided to make her own luck. She went to the racetracks and asked people if she could test their cars to show what she was capable of. A man watched her driving and offered her a chance to race his car.

She was in the Indy 500 just as she had dreamed that she would be. The Indianapolis 500 is the most important race for the type of car she was driving. The race is 200 laps long. For the first 79 laps she was in 4th place. From where she sat, she could see the win in her grasp. She had to pull over, and then found her engine had stalled! For 70 more laps she passed her competitors one by one to get back into the front of the race! With only 10 laps left she was in the lead. 300,000 people in the stadium were on their feet cheering for Danica, men and women alike. As the end neared, her car started to run out of gas. She did not get the win this time, but this race will long be remembered as special.

Danica inspired so many people to believe in what was possible if you put your mind to it. Whether she won or not didn't matter. Sometimes trying can change your life. Today, Danica has many businesses that she runs as a result of how much people love her and the warrior woman that she represents. She believes that if your dreams don't scare you, they aren't big enough.

When it comes to extreme sports, even the professionals use safety equipment. Be sure that you always work with an adult when trying out new sports. You should try and find clubs or teams that focus on the sport you are interested in so that you can try it in a safe and supported environment. Danica started competing at age 10 in a go-kart race, going on to compete in the Indianapolis 500!

Dream of Performing in the Olympics

LIKE

Usain Bolt

I bet you can name all sorts of different types of athletes. Football players, baseball and softball players, tennis players, basketball players—and so many more. The one thing these athletes have in common is extreme self-discipline. Usain Bolt, one of the greatest runners of all time, is an example of how hard work and commitment to your sport can pay off.

Growing up on the island of Jamaica, Usain was interested in many different sports, but running wasn't one of them. When his coach bet him a free lunch that he could not win at a school-sponsored race, he won his free lunch and thus began his love of running. Many people told him despite his speed, his height would be a problem and that his career in running would be brief. He would work very hard to prove them wrong.

Usain still remembers the early days of opening one eye to see his father standing over him, pulling him out of bed. He needed to get up at 4:30 in the morning to be there for 7:00 training. His father was very strict and told him that he should work hard and never be late for a practice. Sometimes only the caretaker would be at the field when he arrived. Soon, those early mornings turned into full days of running with professional coaches. Imagine waking up early every day to run in the tropical heat of Jamaica!

Training to be a professional, for almost every sport, is this demanding. Many hours are spent outside of school in the early morning, evening, and on weekends practicing being the best you can be.

By high school, Usain was running in races, competing with people from all over the world. Looking back, Usain would say,

"If you want to be a winner, you have to work hard from a young age to work for what you want. There are no late bloomers in athletics."

Although Usain was the most famous high school kid in Jamaica because of the races he won and records he set, he was still expected to work hard and be disciplined. One day at school, he witnessed a friend throwing a shoe at a girl and stood by and did nothing. His Dad heard about it, went to the school and punished Usain in front of all of his friends. He believed that being great is not just about having ability, but also having character, a trait that Usain, despite his fame, has always shown to his fans.

His years of hard training paid off when Usain captured something called the "triple triple." This means that he won three gold medals at three different Olympic competitions in a row (2008, 2012, and 2016). This does not just mean hard work as a young man perfecting his speed, but it also means returning home after each Olympic game to start training all over again in anticipation of the next Olympic game 4 years later.

One obvious way to figure out if you have a future as an athlete is to sign up for a sport. Some organizations like the YMCA even have "sampler" programs that let you sample each sport to see if there is one you really like.

What is special about playing sports at a young age is that even if you don't go onto professional sports or to the Olympics like Usain, you will have an excellent habit and there are college scholarships to help pay for your school if you excel at a sport. So get moving!

Dream of Designing Cars
LIKE
Ralph Gilles

Do you have a favorite car? Is it the Volkswagen Beetle because it's small and cute? Is it the Ford Mustang because it's sleek and fast? Or maybe it's a Jeep Wrangler because it's rugged and great for the outdoors? For young Ralph Gilles his favorite car was the Porsche 911. At the age of 11, it was the first car that stood out from other cars on the road. Now Ralph is an industrial designer himself and responsible for the look of many of the cars you see on the road today. Industrial designers like Ralph are responsible for designing products, like cars, furniture or even toys, before they are mass-produced.

As a boy, Ralph negotiated with his parents about doing his homework, but not for the usual reasons. He wanted to be sure that he could watch his favorite "car shows," *Smokey and the Bandit* and *Dukes of Hazard*. He didn't care about the actors but loved to watch the cars on the show. He would study the cars he saw and dream up cars of his own. Hours at a time would go by as he sat in his room with nothing but his notepad and crayons, imagining a different car each time.

One day, his aunt found his drawings and couldn't believe her eyes. "My boy, you have such an artistic gift. You should share it with someone who could help you do this for a living," she told him. Together, they wrote a letter to the head of a car company called Chrysler and included some of his drawings. To his surprise, the head of design wrote him a letter back, praising his drawings and suggesting schools where he might study design.

Years went by and the letter was forgotten as he went off to school to study another subject. He was not happy in his studies and returned home. When he was sad and trying to figure out what he should be doing for a living, he would sit and sketch the same car drawings he did as a kid. His family remembered the letter he received as a child and suggested he look into the schools where he could study industrial car design.

So, Ralph got to it. With only one week to create a dozen drawings to include with his application, Ralph worked day and night to get his portfolio ready. His hard work paid off and he was accepted to the school that would allow him to follow his childhood dream.

Ralph is now the top designer for the company that wrote him that letter all those years ago!

He still feels like he is living that childhood dream as he designs cars for brands he has admired from childhood. "I still pinch myself. Here is a brand I have loved since I was a kid and I get to help design the future of it. I want people decades from now to see the care I put into the design." His job today is to study the car market and analyze how to not only design a beautiful car, but how to solve the problems that cars today do not solve.

What is your dream? Ralph is very happy today that he followed his childhood dream. What can you do to keep yours alive?

If it's being an industrial designer and maybe one day having a car you designed on the road, do something simple like starting an idea journal. Use pictures to explain your ideas and watch over time as they get better and better. Websites like DIY.org and Kidsthinkdesign. org provide inspiration and invite you to upload your pictures and ideas to their website for others to see! Whatever you do, follow Ralph's lead, and keep practicing and working on your ideas so that they will one day come true and not be lost at the bottom of a drawer.

Dream of Designing Landscapes and Pools

LIKE

Lucas Congdon

The next time you walk through a beautiful park, take a moment to appreciate that someone planned how the space would be used for plants, sporting activities, relaxing, and socializing. It's the job of a landscape artist to design how outdoor spaces get used. This applies to public spaces like parks, but also private spaces like people's homes. Lucas Congdon is a landscape artist who can turn a backyard into a unique paradise.

As a child, Lucas and his family didn't have a television and most of his best memories were outside. He grew up roaming the hills of his home state of Vermont. From the age of 4, he would mow the lawn and help his dad in his furniture shop. He was always working with his hands. In order to spend as much time outside as possible, he built a tree house that he was constantly improving. The outdoors was just an extension of his home.

This was just as true at his grandmother's house, whom he called granny. She lived in a u-shaped house with a koi pond in the middle, paths for playing hide and seek, and blueberry bushes that would get raided every morning to be added to his breakfast cereal. No matter where he was, he was always happiest outside. It was no surprise that when, at the age of 10, his mother started her own landscaping company that he wanted to help.

When Lucas was old enough, he set out on his own to start his own landscaping company. He loved being outdoors and creating beautiful spaces for people through his work. However, it wasn't until he was asked by one of his customers to reconstruct their pool that he found his true calling. He immediately shut down his landscaping business and opened "Lucas Lagoons." He didn't want to just build pools; lots of people could do that. He wanted to build dream backyards.

He wanted people to step outside and feel like they were on vacation. Every job he took, he pushed himself to not just deliver a fun backyard, but exceed expectations and deliver something beyond what was expected each and every time. Lucas says, "I really love to know people and know their story. This way I can do more than what is expected. If you deliver more than what people expect, it comes back 10-fold. That is how you really separate yourself. Never feel like you know it all. There is so much you can learn if you have an open mind and open heart."

When you see a backyard that Lucas has designed, one of the things you will notice is his love of rocks. He says, "The rock dictates the design. It's not like building a house with 2x4 pieces of wood. With a rock it is free form and natural. I am not boxed in. You study it and learn all the sides to decide how you will use it. None are the same. Some are so pretty by themselves they become art and others are part of the structure of the pool."

Lucas also really liked making films and even considered studying this in school. As he was getting bigger, crazier, and more creative pool jobs, he began to film his team to show off the before and after. He posted these videos on YouTube and was discovered by someone who turned his videos into a TV show.

Today you can see Lucas putting all of his creativity and love of outdoors to use on the show *Insane Pools*. Lucas's advice to kids who love the outdoors and dream of transforming outdoor spaces is to, "get off your tablets and start using your hands- anything outdoors and creative. Don't be afraid to fail because that is how you get better and better at it." From something as simple as collecting rocks and creating your own rock garden to designing a terrarium, don't be afraid to be creative and get dirty! If you notice a house in your neighborhood that has a great backyard, analyze what makes it so inviting. Take pictures (with the owners' permission) and make a virtual vision board.

Dream of Designing Clothes

LIKE

Donna Karan

Donna Karan was born into the fashion world. Her dad was a well-known tailor and her mom sold and modeled the clothing. Like many children, Donna found her talent because her parents introduced her to the possibility at a young age. Fashion designers are artists who create clothing. They focus on unique designs, how the clothing fits, the color, the shape, the material—every detail is important. Donna Karan became a famous fashion designer and named her clothing line after herself, so people associated these clothes with her.

By the age of 14, Donna was thriving in fashion and participating in fashion shows. However, she was having a rough time in school. She was a visual learner, good at arts and creative subjects, but struggled at other subjects. Donna grew up with attention deficit disorder, which makes it hard to keep focused. She also had dyslexia, which makes it hard to read easily, but no one knew. Since schools usually measure your success by your grades, it was difficult for someone who was artistic, but not skilled in other subjects, to thrive.

Frustrated by this, Donna recalled, "I was not taught to use my imagination or see the world in my own unique way. I was taught to reproduce things that already existed, something I didn't have the skills to do at the time. My intelligence was wrapped up in creativity, self-expression, and street smarts. It didn't occur to me at the time to embrace those qualities. I didn't embrace my creativity, because it made me stand out. I was an oddball. But I grew to own my oddballness."

If you feel that you are best at art based subjects, but school feels hard, art teachers are there to help you. Donna Karan had two art teachers who worked with her and inspired her to focus on the things that she did well. Donna got a job at a teenage clothing store at a very young age. She was good at her job because kids her age came in and she helped them find the right style. She did the same thing for parents who wanted to buy clothing for their children.

Donna believed that learning happens in different ways for different people and she decided the best "school" for her was on-the-job training. She managed to get a job working with a well-known New York designer named Anne Klein who taught her a lifetime's worth of lessons about designing clothes. With those lessons, she began to design her own clothing line named Donna Karan. When deciding whether she was ready to take this leap, her husband told her, "Never be afraid to fail. That is the first step to succeeding."

After that, she designed just seven pieces of clothing. She called them "7 easy pieces." She wanted to make clothes that were easy and went with anything to combine into many different outfits. This idea was very simple, but it was new, and people loved it. She believes this is because she was a designer and not a businessperson. "Business minds look at the past and make small improvements. Designers look to the future and tell you what you need."

Today, because she followed the advice of her art teachers and focused on the things she was good at, Donna Karan has created hundreds of pieces of clothing for men, women, and kids around the world. Her fashion line DKNY is very successful. If you dream of being a fashion designer, there are lots of ways you can practice by learning to sew, creating patterns on plain clothing, or learning to draw your clothing ideas. You can use a toy called "fashion plates" to help get you started. Cut out pictures from magazines of fashion that you like and make a vision board. If you notice someone wearing a cool outfit, ask if you can take their picture and create a collage from your fashion.

22

Dream of Designing the Inside of Homes

LIKE

Joanna Gaines

Joanna Gaines discovered her dream of being an interior decorator after she bought her first home. Wanting to make something special out of a tiny home and a tiny budget, Joanna chose a different theme for each room, using things she found at craft stores and garage sales. When she was decorating her baby's nursery, unable to afford expensive window coverings, she repurposed the type of wood used for a picket fence.

The results were unique and wonderful.

Joanna saw that a tiny budget could be a wonderful design challenge, forcing her to be more creative.

Joanna didn't start out wanting to be an interior decorator. She had a communications degree and hoped to work in television news. She was able to find success, and a television show, in a career for which she had no training because she was able to see the positive aspects of taking a risk. Her motto was, "with change comes new opportunity."

When she and her husband bought an old, broken-down house and they moved in to the fixer upper to sell, Joanna focused on how great the house would look in the end and not how bad it was at the start. She was so inspired by decorating her first home that she opened her own interior decoration store. She ignored those who said she didn't have enough experience and listened to her husband who asked, "why not do it now?"

When the TV show producer called to ask her to be on a reality decorating show, some people thought it was a scam. But, once again, she kept an open mind and called back to find out it was real. Saying "yes" to an opportunity, even if you don't think you're qualified, can result in something wonderful.

What started as redecorating one small house blossomed into a decorating store with thousands of visitors every day. Joanna designed and planned an entire neighborhood full of houses that she and her husband built.

The Gaines were stars of five seasons of a hit TV show. Their dreams were made possible because Joanna saw each challenge as an opportunity to learn and grow. As a designer, her belief today is that spaces should reflect the people living in them. "If all I am doing is creating beautiful spaces, I am failing. But if I'm creating beautiful spaces where families are thriving, then I'm really doing something."

Interior decorators are able to express the mood of a room by choosing objects that send a clear message. Decorators work on many different types of projects. The hotel rooms at Disney World have different themes with objects chosen by a decorator. Do you think your bedroom or playroom is expressing who you are? Do you enjoy setting up the inside of a dollhouse or playhouse?

If you are dreaming of becoming an interior decorator an easy activity is to get pictures of furniture and decorations from magazines or the Internet. Design your own room using scissors and glue. Challenge yourself to repurpose used objects that once seemed old and make them new again, just like Joanna did with the fence boards in her baby's room.

Dream of Designing Art

LIKE

Laolu Senbanjo

Everyone can be an artist. You can use any type of medium to be an artist as well. To make a living as an artist, you have to be brave enough to be different. Laolu Senbanjo showed his bravery by moving across the ocean to put his art everywhere he could think of. He painted on clothing, shoes, guitars, murals, and anywhere he could find to express himself.

When Laolu was a young boy in Nigeria, he would listen to stories from his grandmother. The stories were about Yoruba mythology, an ethnic tribe from the southwestern part of Nigeria. The stories were fascinating to him. His grandmother was covered in tattoos that told the stories of the Yoruba people. He would look up at her tattoos and marvel at them. He thought she was born with these beautiful pictures on her skin. He started to see these pictures everywhere and began to draw them as he saw them. Even when he would see them appear on patterns on their marble floor, he would trace his visions with ink, much to the dismay of his mother.(After getting in trouble for drawing with ink on his floor, he switched to using chalk for his designs).

Laolu's parents weren't convinced that he could make a living as an artist, so they convinced him to go to law school. However, his notebooks would end up full of the Yoruba drawings that he made as a child and not the lessons from class.

During his time in law school, he was able to work as a human rights attorney (someone who defends the rights of people who may not be able to do it for themselves). During this time he learned about people being treated badly. The only way he could work through his sadness and frustration was through his art.

Using his art he was able paint a picture of the things he saw and the joys and the sadness of the people he was helping. The more he painted and drew, the more he felt that art was still his true calling. He packed up his supplies and left Africa for New York City. He had no money, no studio to paint in, and no place to sell his art, so he just started painting on anything he could find. He stared with shirts and shoes and he found that people actually loved wearing his art. He moved to other objects that people would bring him and he would create custom art for them based on the story he wanted to tell.

One day, as he was looking at Instagram, he saw someone posing in front of his art and the art seemed to become one with her body. This made him think, "If the art on my grandmother was so beautiful, the body can become another canvas for me to work with."

One day, Laolu got an email asking him to use his art as part of a music video. The letter read, "Hello, would you like to paint for my music video? Signed, Beyoncé." He immediately deleted the email because he assumed it was a scam. However, it was true and his art was featured in the music video "Lemonade." After that, people started to recognize his art and him as an artist. Laolu says that while it is a blessing to be recognized as an artist, his true goal is to continue to fight for the things he believes in and to help people get to know Africa better. "Africa is not one big place," Laolu says, "There are over 350 ethnic groups and languages and I am just one of them."

To be a great artist, you need to be able to think like Laolu in order to create art you believe in that is different. Not everyone will like every piece of art and that is okay. If your art is different enough, many people will love it. One great way to be inspired as a budding artist is to go to a craft store like Hobby Lobby or Michaels and walk the aisles. Look at the different types of materials and art styles. What excites you? Is there a topic you care a lot about to help inspire the topic of your art? Whatever it is, simply dare to be different.

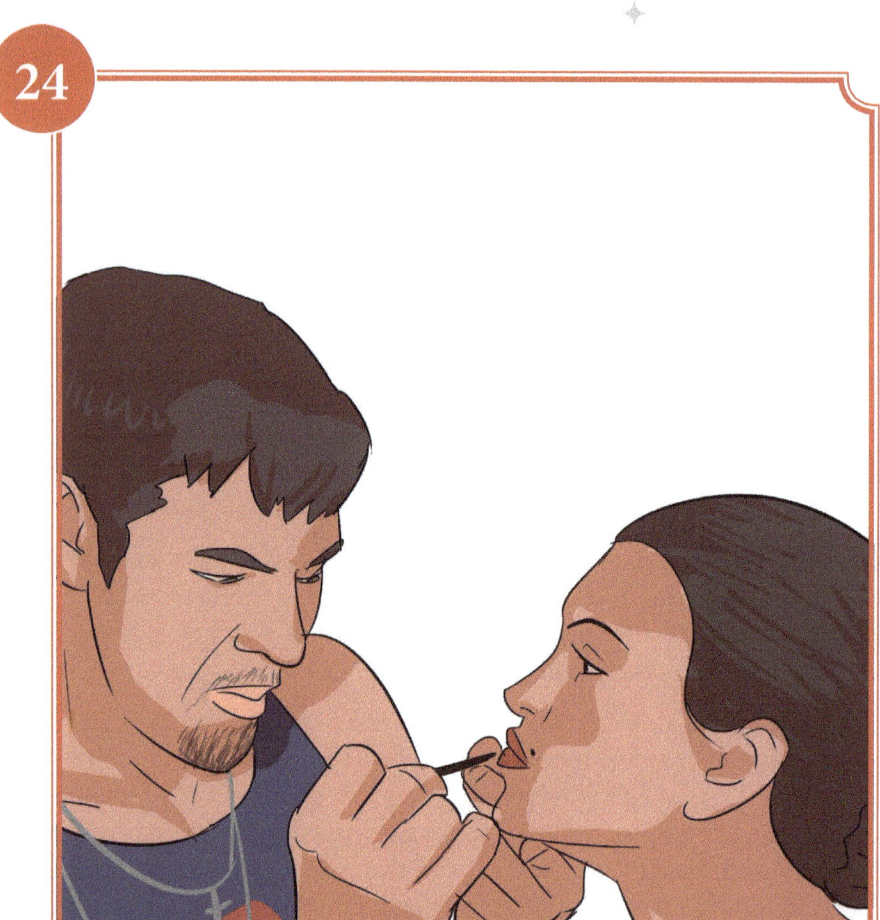

Dream of Designing on Faces

LIKE

Kevyn Aucoin

Making people feel beautiful and look their best can be a rewarding job. Whether it is preparing someone for a big day, like a wedding, helping actresses and models to look their best in front of a camera, or completely transforming someone to have a brand-new look, makeup artists do all of this. Kevyn Aucoin grew to be one of the most famous makeup artists, working with some of the biggest celebrities and super models. It all started in his living room as an 11-year-old child.

An 11-year-old Kevyn ran around his house gathering up his sisters and placing them in chairs. "You are my models!" he said trying out different looks on them. It was his favorite way to be creative. "It made me feel like I had something special to offer the world."

Kevyn knew that he was different from the other boys in his school and it caused him to be an outsider. He was teased and made to feel unwelcome, so he agreed with his parents that he should transfer to a beauty school where he could continue to develop his skill and passion for makeup.

Kevyn's dad was very proud of him and said, "Kevyn pretty much taught the class on applying makeup because he was such an artist. A woman, to Kevyn, was a canvas and he was just an artist painting a picture. He could look at any woman and see her beauty, whether she saw it or not."

He quickly realized that he needed to be in New York City where there were many more opportunities to work his magic on models and actresses. This is how he got his first big break by offering to make up models for free in order to add their pictures to his portfolio and show off his work. Models loved working with him and one day someone at a very famous magazine saw his pictures and realized how good he was.

It was very clever of Kevyn to do his early work for free because this gave him experience and exposure in a world where no one knew who he was.

Do you have something you are passionate about doing? Do you love animals? You can volunteer at a shelter or walk a neighbor's dog in order to gain experience. When it comes time to be paid for your work, you will have people who can recommend you.

If helping people feel better about themselves through exploring makeup techniques seems interesting to you, there are lots of ways you can practice. You can practice on friends and siblings like Kevyn did. Styling is another skill that you should learn if you want to work in the world of beauty. Buy a "hair model" and practice learning braids, updo's, and different hairdos. There are lots of YouTube videos to give you tips and advice on different styles of makeup and hair that you can practice doing.

Take advice from Kevyn and take pictures of your styles and save them to show off your work and track how you get better!

Dream of Designing Cartoons

LIKE

Bill Peet

Bill Peet dreamed of being an artist, but did not realize his dream of becoming an illustrator until he worked at Disney Studios for over a year. When Bill was a child, he was rarely seen without his sketchbook. He hid in the attic to draw or went to the woods or his family's farm to create funny versions of the animals he saw there. When the travelling zoo came to town, he spent hours sketching the exotic animals. Little did he know that one day he would be drawing an elephant named Dumbo that children around the world would instantly love.

Bill's passion for drawing did not always serve him well in school. He got in trouble with his teacher for doodling characters instead of paying attention. Despite poor grades, he remained focused and followed his love of art. In high school he was allowed to take art classes. By improving his skills, he won a scholarship to an art school hoping to be a painter.

Bill needed a reliable job while he built his reputation as a painter. One day at art school, he was asked to come audition at Disney as an "in-betweening artist". The process was almost like a competitive reality TV show. Each day an artist would be eliminated until only the best ones were left.

An in-betweening artist refines the work that comes after the main artist is done. The main artist draws a Mickey Mouse story and then the "in-betweening artist" finishes the pictures needed to fill in the story and make the motion of the cartoon, seamless. It was a hard job, without any credit in the final product, but Bill persisted in the hope of getting important projects that better reflected his talent.

After he proved himself as an "in-betweening artist," Bill started to submit small character ideas. Eventually he was asked to draw full scenes for *Snow White*, and then actually write a scene for *Dumbo* and *Peter Pan*. After continuing to take on better assignments, Walt Disney asked him to turn the book, *101 Dalmatians*, into a movie! Bill said, "It was a wonder I could write much more than my own name after drawing and daydreaming through my English classes in grade school and high school." But he did. He worked on other projects as well like *Sleeping Beauty*, *The Sword in the Stone* and *The Jungle Book*.

Bill found success drawing cartoons at Disney for 27 years because he took on jobs when he was young that seemed dull or thankless. He had talent equal to those who were drawing more important characters, but he had to prove to Walt Disney how much talent he had, even if it took years. Sometimes, while pursuing our dreams, we have to start at the bottom and work to prove our skills to others.

If you like to draw, being an illustrator might be a wonderful career for you. There are graphic novels that tell a story with tons of pictures and jobs in the legal profession illustrating a trial. You can even be a tattoo artist! There are lots of ways to practice your illustration skills like creating your own book by stapling pieces of paper together, trying to copy the illustrations out of your favorite books, or finding step-by-step books or videos to learn to draw new objects and characters. Whatever you do, just start drawing!

26

Dream of Designing Photographs

LIKE

Anne Geddes

It's hard to believe that something we can do 100 times a day with our phones is also something you can do for a living. But taking great pictures is harder than you think and it's required for lots of things like events, magazines, newspapers, and personal use.

Anne Geddes is a professional photographer who said, "My story is about confidence. I learned from my mistakes and they helped to grow my style." In high school, Anne travelled to another country and realized how much she loved taking pictures.

Her first act of confidence after finishing college was to move to Hong Kong and to start taking pictures of local families. Anne used her husband's old camera and learned how to use it on the job. Other than personal photos, she had no experience taking professional photos. She didn't have a photo studio or any training, but she loved photography and thought she might be good at it. She took her camera and put an ad up in the local supermarket and waited for people to call. Today she looks back and would tell other new photographers about being inexperienced, "never hesitate to admit how green you are because green signifies new life and growth."

Taking pictures of families in Hong Kong is where Anne discovered her love of photographing children. She realized how few pictures she had of herself as a child and as a result, how little of her personality emerged in those photos. She didn't just want to capture the image of children. She wanted to capture their "individual character."

Anne thought that normal professional portraits of young children were boring and lacked personality. They mainly showed children wearing their best clothes, often looking embarrassed and uncomfortable, or just plain bored.

Many people told Anne that limiting her pictures to children was a bad idea, but Anne opened her "children only" studio in her garage anyway. In order to keep pushing her creativity, once a month, Anne would do a free photoshoot of babies put into all sorts of creative settings. For example, for one of her first shoots, she dressed up babies like little cabbages. Her craziest photoshoot was one that made her famous. She took 123 babies and put them into flowerpots and took their picture with their heads popping out. She had great skill with lighting and creating unique settings but imagine getting 123 babies to sit still?

Anne entered these unique photographs into contests and won! Her success increased her self-confidence. Anne believes that you need to, "go forward in your way of thinking and find how you will do your own art in your own unique way."

As proof of the confidence she had gained, she used her savings to turn her pictures into greeting cards and calendars. Today, these cards and calendars are in 79 countries and translated into 23 languages and she is one of the best-known photographers in the world. Anne now uses this fame to bring attention to issues that directly impact children, believing that "babies are our eternal chance at a new beginning."

Today it is a lot easier to practice being a photographer with digital photography. A fun game to play is a "photo scavenger hunt." Have someone create a list of objects and then take a camera or phone and find them. Use light, filters, and angles to create cool images. Be confident like Anne and try different ways of creating your visual story.

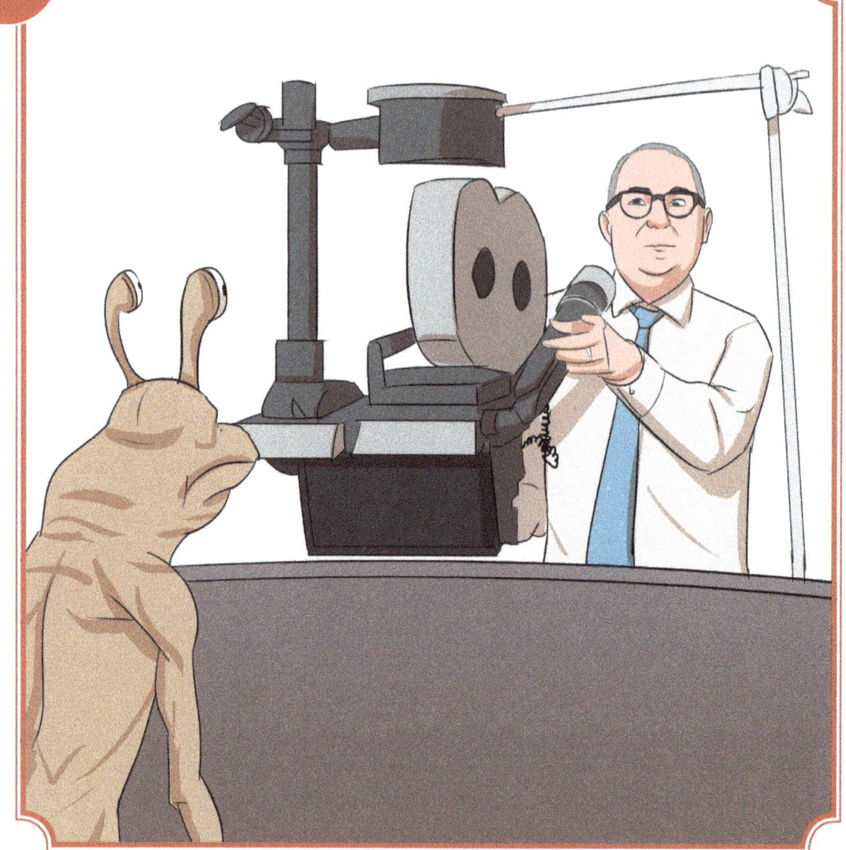

27

Dream of Directing the Design of a Movie

LIKE

Barry Sonnenfeld

A director is the person who is in charge of how the film looks. All movies start off as a script, sort of like a book or a play. It is the director's job to figure out how to change that script into a story told in words and images. A director chooses the actors who represent the characters, the setting of the movie, the way the actors play the characters, and how the story comes together in the end. The director is the "boss" of a movie.

It is funny to think about, but Barry Sonnenfeld found his way to making movies because of a book. When he was young, he fell in love with a novel called *On the Road*. The book was about carefree friends that traveled around the United States having adventures. He wanted to be like the author and hit the open road, write stories, and take pictures. It was this love of taking pictures that started his career. Think about this, the power a book had on the life and decisions of a person.

Every young person has access to a library and can start learning about other people and interests. You don't have to wait until you graduate from high school or college to find your passion. In fact, Barry didn't wait to grow up. Barry turned his childhood bedroom into a darkroom to practice his photography skills.

What started as a kid with a photography hobby turned into a career directing movies like The *Addams Family* and *Men in Black*. This progression was a result of being open to major career opportunities when they presented themselves. Barry says about his career that, "a miracle is what seems impossible, but happens anyway—that sums up my life."

After Barry spent years working in the photography field, his mother suggested that he go to film school since running a film camera, in her opinion, was a way to put all his images together. Although that isn't really how cinematography works, he enrolled in film school. Because he was willing to thinking about his interest in photography in a different way, new opportunities opened up.

While in film school, he made friends with two filmmaking brothers, the Coen brothers, and he ran the camera as a cinematographer, while the brothers directed. This was the Coen's first movie and they continued to work together as a team, becoming more famous with each new movie. Barry viewed being in charge of the camera as more than just a job. He thought about it as being a friend and a second pair of eyes for the directors. Making a movie is about working with other people.

One day, someone who wanted to make a movie called *The Addams Family* approached Barry. They did not want Barry to run the camera; they wanted him to be the "boss" or the director! Barry couldn't understand why they would want someone without any directing experience. The movie needed to be artistic and have a very special look, someone who understood how to shoot film and guide a script to be its best. Barry's willingness to consider another major career change meant he had other opportunities to direct movies that became famous, like *The Adams Family* and *Men in Black*.

If being the cameraman or the director of a movie sounds like fun, there are apps or programs, like Magisto, that you can download today to start practicing making movies. You can also find movie making kits that help you make animated movies. LEGO Movie Maker kit allows you to create movie-like scenes using a "movie-making" app, LEGO characters, and scenery. You can experience the different roles that a director plays and imagine yourself being the "boss" of a movie.

28

Dream of Editing the Design of a Movie

LIKE

Maryann Brandon

When a movie is shot, the director collects hundreds of hours of film to be sure that all the right angles and acting shots are captured. However, as you know, movies are not hundreds of hours. It's someone's job to take all of that film and make it into a movie. This person is called a movie editor. Maryann Brandon (and her editing partner Mary Jo Markey) edited *Star Wars: The Force Awakens* and were responsible for making the story come to life.

When Maryann was young, she would go to the movie theater on Saturdays and watch not one, not two, but three movies in a row. She would spend the whole day in the theater taking in the movie and falling in love with each story, especially James Bond. She saw every James Bond film the moment it came out.

In film school, she had to do all of the parts of making a movie including writing, filming, and editing. When she got to the editing stage, she didn't have anyone to help her so she got a job at a place where they edited movies and in exchange she was given access to the tools she needed to edit her movie. "Wow," Maryann thought, "This is really fun. I like seeing how the story all comes together at the end. I like that this is where the final movie happens!" She was mesmerized by how magic could be made out of a mess and knew that this is where she was meant to be.

As Maryann began editing, she was working on TV shows. However, her real dream was to edit movies. When the director that she had been working with on the TV show went on to make his first movie, Maryann was beyond excited. "This is my chance!" she thought, "I am going to be a movie editor." As her excitement continued to build, a dark cloud came over hear dream. "Someone else might get the job, someone who would be brand new to our team! This is so unfair," Maryann silently thought to herself and she stormed out of her office. That night, it hit her. Had she actually said she was interested in the job? Had she even mentioned her dream to anyone else?

The next day, she found the director in the parking lot and shared her dream with him. He gave her the job and they have been working on movies together ever since, including *Star Wars: The Force Awakens.*

When working on the *Star Wars* movie, she started working before the movie even started filming. Because of her close relationship with the director, she sat on the set and edited while the movie was being filmed. "I was part of the crew, getting to know the cast and what they were going for, really helped me get it right," said Maryann. One time she was a bit surprised to be editing and she looked up and saw Chewbacca leaning over her shoulder watching!

Maryann suggests that this is a great career for people who like labor-intensive projects that you can work on by yourself. "It's very rewarding if you can stick to it and concentrate on something for a very long time."

She would also remind young women to remember to ask for the things that you want, just as she did when she wanted to work on her first movie. "If you don't ask, you won't get it."

It is much easier now for people to edit their own movies, right on their own device. Pay attention to music videos you watch. You'll notice that it changes the direction you see things from. This is done by the editor. Practice your skills on a music video. Tape yourself (or someone else) lip-syncing to a song, but film it a few times from a few different angles. Then, use editing software to try and edit the shots together to make only one video that changes between multiple angles.

Dream of Designing Concert/Theater Sets

LIKE

Es Devlin

When you go to a concert or a play, the person in charge of bringing the story's environment to life that you see on the stage is the set designer. Set designers work with the people performing on stage to figure out the best way to bring the show to life. For Es Devlin, this career combined music and creativity, her two favorite things.

Es lived outside of a big city, London, and when she was 11, her parents allowed her to go into the city on her own for music lessons. After her lessons, Es would wander the city taking in the sights and the sounds. Her favorite thing to do on these afternoons alone was to see a live music show. She would find a new band or artist to see, buy her ticket and step inside the venue, so excited to be a part of the music scene. When she stood in the back of the room taking it all in, she was surprised that each show seemed exactly the same. She would think to herself, "Why are all these shows the same. Why are they not more exciting to watch?" Es thought a concert should be as much for your eyes as your ears!

Es's parents encouraged her creativity and gave her toy theaters to play with and taught her how to turn "junk" into usable items for the house. In fact, their family dinner table was made out of old scaffolding planks. Despite this, it didn't occur to her that her desire to see more exciting concerts and her love for her puppet theaters would one day come together to create a career.

Es went off to college with the same love of design and music that she had as a child but was still unsure of what to path to take. She did what a lot of new college students do by taking different classes to try and figure it out. She found her passion in a theater design class. In fact, her class project went so well that she won a prize and was invited to work on her first professional play!

Es started in a very small theater, where she said it felt like "close up magic." They used all sorts of junk for the set design and Es would paint, mold, and weld to transform the space, just like her parents had taught her years ago. One of her first projects in this very small theater was to make it rain inside of a small room.

Her real break came when she designed for her first band. She thought back to all the shows she saw as a child and wanted to make something that the eyes could enjoy as much as the ears. Es constructed a huge box for each band member to play in so that they would stand out on their own. The famous singer, Kanye West, saw this and thought her idea was so creative that he hired her to design the stage for his next concert. You can see her design in the drawing behind her picture.

These stages are so elaborate they are considered large scale touring sculptures. Es has created these stage sculptures in collaboration with Beyoncé,

Kanye West, Adele, U2, The Weekend, Lorde, Pet Shop Boys, and the Royal Opera House in London. For each of these artists, Es has to absorb every word that an artist sings and ask herself, "What should be around them when they are saying this?" then she designs a stage and setting best suited for what the artist is singing.

Es says that her art is different because, "My type of art is built with the knowledge that it will only last a short time. When people see my sets during a show it will only exist that one time in that one way and will only live on in people's memories."

Similar to the toys that Es played with as a child, you can practice designing your own sets with puppet theaters. You can use something as simple as a cereal box and cut out a hole and focus on decorating the foreground and background. How will your decorations bring to life the story you want to tell?

DREAM IT & do it

100 POSSIBILITIES, STORIES, REAL-LIFE ROLE MODELS.

FOR GIRLS AND BOYS

INSPIRING ALL THE THINGS YOU CAN BE

HOLLY A. SHARP

www.ingramcontent.com/pod-product-compliance
Lightning Source LLC
Chambersburg PA
CBHW040857070726
47599CB00035B/2026